NATIONAL FORUM ON EUROPE
FÓRAM NÁISIÚNTA UM AN EORAIP

A SUMMARY GUIDE TO
THE TREATY OF LISBON
(EU REFORM TREATY)

JANUARY 2008

NATIONAL FORUM ON EUROPE
FÓRAM NÁISIÚNTA UM AN EORAIP

Published by the Stationery Office, Dublin

To be purchased directly from the Government Publications Office,
Sun Alliance House, Molesworth Street, Dublin 2

Or by mail order from Government Publications,
Postal Trade Section, 51 St. Stephen's Green, Dublin 2
(Tel. 01 6476834/35/36/37: Fax: 01 6476843)

Or through any bookseller.

Designed by Austin Butler (austinbutler@mac.com)

€ 1

TABLE OF CONTENTS

Foreword   1

Background to the Treaty   3

Summary Guide   5

Introduction   7

Structure of the Treaty   9

Values and Objectives   11

EU Institutions   13

EU Powers and Decisionmaking   20

Decisionmaking   22

Enhanced Cooperation   27

Common Foreign and Security Policy   28

Freedom, Security and Justice   31

Charter of Fundamental Rights   34

Changes in Economic Governance Field   39

Procedure for Future Amendments   40

Clauses of General Application   42

Adoption, Ratification and Entry into Force
of the Treaty of Lisbon   43

Glossary of Treaty Terms   44

Summary List of New Areas
for Qualified Majority Voting (QMV)   58

Comparison with the European Constitution   65

Earlier EU Treaties   66

EU Treaty and Enlargement History (Timeline)   71

FOREWORD

*By the Independent Chairman of the National Forum On Europe,
Maurice Hayes*

This year, the people of Ireland will again have their say on a
European treaty. The National Forum On Europe has worked
since 2002 to promote a public debate on the EU and on
Ireland's role in Europe. In pursuit of its mandate, the Forum
has published a series of documents and audio-visual materials
in plain language that could be understood by the citizen.

This user-friendly document offers a guide to the latest EU
treaty, the Treaty of Lisbon, also known as the Reform Treaty.
This Summary Guide is prefaced by a short explanation
of the background to this Treaty, including the European
Constitution (2004) which will not come into force.

There is a great need for a reliable and readable guide to this new
Treaty which is lengthy and complex. The effects of the new
Treaty, which operates by amending the existing Treaties, can
only be understood in relation to the existing EU arrangements
and changes in one area can impact on other areas.

The Summary Guide aims to be factual and does not make
judgements on the various elements. A considerable amount
of selection was unavoidable in the interests of brevity. While
it has not been possible, therefore, to reflect fully all aspects
of the treaty, the Summary Guide has sought to cover the
most important elements, especially from Ireland's point
of view. Technical language is avoided where possible and a
glossary is provided for technical terms which are used. We
have also included a comparison between the key features of
the European Constitution and the new Treaty.

The role of the National Forum On Europe is not to advocate
any particular policy or course of action but rather to
generate debate and to provide an arena for inclusive
dialogue on matters relating to Ireland's role in Europe.
Our website, *www.forumoneurope.ie*, provides easy access to
information about the European Union and about our work
over the past six years. You will find clear and user- friendly
guides to the EU's work and institutions.

This publication is offered in that spirit as the Irish people prepare to decide on this new Treaty. I hope that it will be accepted as objective information for the public and that it will help people to understand and to discuss the very important matters with which it deals.

I wish to express my appreciation for the work done by the Forum's Secretariat and all those who helped prepare this publication.

BACKGROUND TO THE TREATY

The fundamental rules and institutions of the EU are set out in treaties agreed among the Member States. As the EU developed and responded to changing circumstances over the past 50 years, the process of change to these rules and institutions required a series of treaties.

The most recent Treaty to come into effect, the Treaty of Nice, made changes to the EU institutions prior to the accession of ten new Member States in 2004.

After the Treaty of Nice, the European Council, adopted a Declaration which posed a series of targeted questions on the future of the Union, around four main themes: the division and definition of powers, the simplification of the treaties, the institutional set-up and moving towards a Constitution for European citizens.

One year later, the Convention on the Future of Europe was established to consider the key issues for the future development of an enlarged EU and to identify the various possible responses.

The Convention was made up of 205 members headed by its President, Valéry Giscard d'Estaing, former President of France. Its members were representatives of Governments and national parliaments from EU Member States and the then candidate countries, together with representatives of the European Parliament and the European Commission.

The Convention on the Future of Europe completed its work in July 2003 when it presented its "Draft Treaty establishing a Constitution for Europe" to the Council of Ministers.

Negotiations seeking agreement on the draft European Constitution began with an Inter-Governmental Conference (IGC) in October 2003 and were completed in June 2004 during Ireland's EU Presidency when all elements of the proposed European Constitution were agreed.

The European Constitution sought to consolidate all previous treaties in a single text and to make significant changes. The European Constitution could only come into effect if and when ratified by all Member States.

Before Ireland proceeded with its referendum on the European Constitution, referendums in France (May 2005) and in the Netherlands (June 2005) resulted in "No" votes. In response, the European Council called for a "period of reflection", during which a broad debate would take place in each Member State, involving citizens, civil society, social partners, national Parliaments and political parties. This period was used by the National Forum On Europe as a period, not only of reflection, but also of engagement.

In March 2007, Heads of State and Government of the European Union met in Berlin and adopted a Declaration on the 50th Anniversary of the Treaty of Rome, which laid the foundation for today's EU. In the Declaration, the leaders of Europe were "united in our aim of placing the European Union on a renewed common basis before the European Parliament elections in 2009".

The German Presidency presented a report at the June 2007 European Council based on extensive consultations with Member States about the future of Europe. In response, the European Council agreed a detailed mandate for an Inter-Governmental Conference (IGC) to prepare a new Treaty. The IGC was asked to draw up a Treaty amending the existing European Treaties with a view to enhancing the enlarged EU's

- efficiency and democratic legitimacy, and
- the coherence of its external action.

The IGC mandate provided that the new Treaty would be based upon the existing Treaties and it would not have "constitutional characteristics". The mandate specified a number of ways in which the new Treaty would differ from the Constitution but, otherwise, the new Treaty would incorporate almost all the other innovations proposed in the European Constitution.

The final text of the Treaty drawn up by the IGC was approved in the margins of the informal European Council in Lisbon on 18-19 October and signed on behalf of the Member States on 13 December 2007. The signing of the Treaty will be followed by ratification processes in all 27 countries. The new Treaty could come into force as early as 1 January 2009 but it will not come into force unless and until it is ratified by all 27 Member States.

SUMMARY GUIDE

- Introduction
- Some Key Points of the Treaty
- Structure of the Treaty
- Values and Objectives
- EU Institutions
- EU Powers and Decisionmaking
- Decisionmaking
- Enhanced Cooperation
- Common Foreign and Security Policy
- Freedom, Security and Justice
- Charter of Fundamental Rights
- Changes in Economic Governance Field
- Procedure for Future Amendments
- Clauses of General Application
- Adoption, Ratification and Entry into Force of the Treaty of Lisbon

INTRODUCTION

In order to highlight the Treaty's important features, the Summary Guide does not follow the lay-out of the Treaty but it aims to mention its key features. The Summary Guide does not offer a legal interpretation of the Treaty of Lisbon and, where it mentions a specific Treaty provision, its account may omit some features in the interests of brevity.

The time-line attached to this Summary Guide shows the dates of each Treaty and other major EU developments, particularly the enlargements of the EU.

Some Key Points of the Treaty

* Qualified majority voting (QMV) will become the normal rule for the Council of Ministers. National vetoes will be removed in many areas (summary list in appendix);

* Decisions by qualified majority (QMV) will require a "double majority" in the Council (55 per cent of Member States representing 65 per cent of the EU's population);

* The European Parliament will gain co-decision powers in many policy areas;

* A European Council President will chair the European Council for up to five years;

* A High Representative of the Union for Foreign Affairs and Security Policy will combine two existing jobs - Vice-President of the Commission and High Representative for Foreign and Security Policy;

* The number of Commissioners will be reduced (each Member State would have a Commissioner for two out of every three terms);

* The number of MEPs is set at a maximum of 750, plus the Parliament's President (with a minimum of six and a maximum of 96 MEPs per country);

* National parliaments get the right to raise objections against draft EU legislation where national or local action would be more effective;

* The EU is given a single legal personality;

* An exit clause provides procedures for Member States wishing to leave the EU;

* Asylum, immigration, police and judicial cooperation will no longer have a separate status ("pillar") but Ireland, with the UK, will have an opt-out/opt-in;

* Foreign and Security Policy is integrated with other areas of the EU but special procedures still apply, including unanimity for policy decisions;

* The Treaty maintains full respect for Ireland's policy of military neutrality. It mandates Member States to increase their own military capabilities with a view to increasing the capabilities available for the EU's Common Security and Defence Policy;

* New challenges, such as climate change and energy solidarity, are recognised;

* A Protocol is added on services of general interest, including economic services of general interest;

* The EU is given greater controls in the area of macro economic policy and additional tools to curb Member States with excessive budget deficits;

* New procedures provide for simplified Treaty revisions in certain specified areas.

* The Charter of Fundamental Rights is given Treaty status.

STRUCTURE OF THE TREATY

The Treaty of Lisbon (EU Reform Treaty), if ratified by the Member States, will operate by amending the two treaties that embody the EU's fundamental rules.

These are

- the Treaty on European Union (TEU) i.e. the Maastricht Treaty (1992), as amended;
- the Treaty establishing the European Community i.e. the Treaty of Rome (1957) as amended. Its title will change to the Treaty on the Functioning of the European Union (TFEU).

The new Treaty will change the format of both the existing Treaties.

The Treaty on European Union (TEU) will have six parts,

Title I	Common Provisions
Title II	Democratic Principles
Title III	Institutions
Title IV	Enhanced Cooperation
Title V	External Actions and Common Foreign and Security Policy
Title VI	Final Provisions

Title II on Democratic Principles and Title III on Institutions are new, although many of their provisions reflect existing rules, and the provisions on Freedom, Security and Justice have been moved to the Treaty on the Functioning of the European Union.

The Treaty on the Functioning of the European Union (TFEU), which will contain the detailed rules on the workings of the EU, will have the following format:

Part One	Principles
Part Two	Non-discrimination and citizenship of the Union
Part Three	Union Policies and Internal Actions
Parts Four	Overseas Countries and Territories
Part Five	External Action by the Union

Part Six Institutional and Budgetary Provisions

Part Seven General and Final Provisions

The bulk of the Treaty is contained in Part Three and Part Six. A notable change in the Treaty's structure is the addition of Part Five dealing with the EU's external action, which is linked to Title V of the Treaty on European Union (TEU).

The Lisbon (Reform) Treaty also contains a series of Protocols and a number of Declarations have been made regarding the Treaty. A number of these protocols and declarations are directly relevant to Ireland, particularly the protocol and declaration relating to the Irish and UK opt-out on judicial cooperation in criminal matters and police cooperation (detailed below).

An important effect of the new Treaty will be to abolish the EU's current structure of three "Pillars". The First Pillar is based on the Treaty establishing the European Community, which includes the Single Market. First Pillar decisionmaking normally involves a proposal from the Commission with a qualified majority vote in the Council. The role of the European Parliament depends on the nature of the proposal.

The Second Pillar deals with the Common Foreign and Security Policy while the Third Pillar deals with Police and Judicial Cooperation in criminal matters. The second and third pillars have inter-governmental procedures with national vetoes for most decisions and a limited role for the European Parliament.

The Treaty would abolish this inter-governmental pillar system while retaining special voting procedures for the Common Foreign and Security Policy.

The nature of the European Union's Second and Third Pillars has given rise to questions about its legal status. Under the new Treaty, the European Union replaces the European Community and the existing European Union with a single legal personality which has treaty-making powers.

VALUES AND OBJECTIVES

Drawing largely on the provisions in the European Constitution, the new Treaty sets out the values on which the EU is founded and which are common to the Member States.

In a society in which pluralism, non-discrimination, tolerance, justice, solidarity and equality between women and men prevail, these values are

- human dignity;
- liberty;
- democracy;
- equality;
- the rule of law;
- respect for human rights, including the rights of persons belonging to minorities.

While the Treaty does not adopt the Constitution's preamble, it does add a paragraph from the Constitution to the existing Treaty on European Union preamble on the values which have developed from Europe's "cultural, religious and humanist inheritance".

Article 3 of the Treaty on European Union will set out the basic aim of the EU – "to promote peace, its values and the well-being of its peoples" – and a set of overall objectives for the EU.

The Charter of Fundamental Rights, which sets out the civil, political, economic and social rights recognised by the EU, is given Treaty status. (Details below).

Membership of the EU

In considering any application for membership of the EU, the new Treaty requires the conditions of eligibility agreed upon by the European Council to be taken into account. This refers to the "Copenhagen criteria" which are:

- stability of institutions guaranteeing democracy, the rule of law, human rights and respect for and, protection of minorities;
- the existence of a functioning market economy as well as the capacity to cope with competitive pressure and market forces within the Union;

- the candidate's ability to take on the obligations of membership including adherence to the aims of political, economic and monetary union.

Voluntary Withdrawal

The new Treaty introduces a procedure for voluntary withdrawal from the EU. Should a Member State decide to withdraw, it would notify the Council of its decision. The EU would then negotiate an agreement with the Member State concerned, detailing the arrangements for the withdrawal and outlining the relationship between the Member State and the EU after withdrawal. That agreement would be concluded on behalf of the EU by the Council, acting by QMV, after obtaining the assent of the European Parliament. The withdrawing State would not participate in the Council's discussions or decisions concerning it.

EU INSTITUTIONS

The Treaty adds both the European Council and the European Central Bank to the existing institutions of the European Union. These institutions are designed to promote the EU's values, and to advance its objectives, and interests. The EU will therefore be served by the following seven institutions working in co-operation:

- The European Parliament;
- The European Council;
- The Council;
- The European Commission;
- The Court of Justice of the European Union;
- The European Central Bank;
- The Court of Auditors.

Detailed arrangements for the working of each institution are set out in the Treaty on the Functioning of the European Union (TFEU).

The European Parliament

The new Treaty gives the European Parliament a significantly enhanced role. The Parliament will exercise legislative and budgetary powers jointly with the Council and it will exercise functions of political control and consultation as laid down in the Treaties.

The Parliament will elect the President of the Commission – at present, its assent is required for this appointment).

It will have a maximum of 750 members plus its President (compared to 732 normally at present). Each Member State will have at least six Members of the European Parliament (MEPs) and no Member State will have more than 96. Within these limits, national representation will be broadly in proportion to population but with more favourable treatment for the smaller Member States.

Under the Nice Treaty, seats were allocated to take account of the new Member States. Ireland was allocated 12 seats but received an additional temporary seat because Bulgaria and Romania did not join in 2004. The European Council recently agreed on an allocation of seats, based on a proposal by the Parliament, for the 2009 elections. Ireland will have 12 seats - the same number as provided for under the Nice Treaty.

The European Council

The European Council gives the EU its political direction and sets its priorities. It is made up of the most senior political representatives of the Member States – Prime Ministers and Presidents with executive powers. The President of the European Commission is also a member of the European Council. The European Council, which does not have power to make laws, normally makes its decisions by unanimity.

The Treaty creates a new position of "President of the European Council" who will chair its meetings, drive forward its work and represent the EU abroad at the highest level.

This new position will replace the current system where the European Council is chaired by the Member State holding the rotating six-month Presidency of the EU Council. The European Council will meet at least four times a year (which is the current practice although it is only required to meet twice a year).

The European Council will elect its President by a qualified majority vote for a term of $2^1/2$ years, renewable once (i.e. a maximum of five years). This term can be ended by the European Council in the event of an impediment or serious misconduct. The President of the European Council cannot hold any national position - a serving Prime Minister or Head of State, for example, could not hold this post.

The Council

The Council, which is made up of government ministers representing the Member States, will be the key decisionmaking body, along with the European Parliament.

Under the new Treaty, the Council will continue to be made up of one Government Minister from every Member State.

The European Council will decide on what will in future be the other council formations, e.g. agriculture ministers, environment ministers, etc. . However, a new post, the High Representative of the Union for Foreign Affairs and Security Policy, is being created to permanently chair the Foreign Affairs Council.

The High Representative of the Union for Foreign Affairs and Security Policy would also represent the EU in the political, diplomatic, trade and aid arenas. This post will replace the two people who cover these areas now - as Vice-President of the Commission, for the trade and aid aspects, and secondly, reporting to the Foreign Affairs Council on the political and diplomatic aspects.

A new European External Action Service (an EU Diplomatic Corps) will be established to support the High Representative's work.

The Presidency of the other Council formations will be held by Member State representatives on the basis of strict rotation (currently, the Presidency rotates every six months; there are plans for a team system with three Member States sharing the Presidency for an 18 month period).

The Council will have a new voting system (see section on Decisionmaking) and will meet in public when it is considering or voting on legislation.

The European Commission

The Commission is intended to represent the interests of the EU as a whole. The Commission:

- is the only EU institution with the power to initiate the laws on which the European Parliament and Council have to take a decision;
- administers the budget and manages the Community programmes;
- seeks to ensure that EU treaties, laws, rules and decisions are complied with;
- negotiates for the EU in the international trade and aid areas;
- is independent from and does not seek instruction from any government or other body.

All this would continue but there will be important changes to the Commission's membership.

Currently,

- each of the 27 Member States has one of its nationals as a Commissioner;

- the Council of Ministers, meeting at the level of Heads of State or Government, nominates the Commission's President-elect, deciding by QMV;
- the Council of Ministers, again by QMV, agrees the list of Commissioners nominated by the Member States;
- the full nominated Commission is submitted to the European Parliament for a vote of approval.

Under the Treaty, the system would change from November 2009. The Commission would be made up of one national from each Member State, including its President.

The President of the Commission would be nominated by the European Council, acting on the basis of QMV, and elected by the European Parliament.

The High Representative of the Union for Foreign Affairs and Security Policy would also be a Vice-President of the Commission.

And from 2014:

The Commission would comprise a number of members corresponding to two-thirds of the Member States (unless the European Council, acting unanimously, decides otherwise). The Commissioners will be selected on the basis of equal rotation between Member States. In effect, each Member State would have a national serving as Commissioner for ten years out of every fifteen.

Once this new system takes effect, for the first time, the European Parliament would be entitled to elect or reject the nominee for Commission President. In the case of rejection, the procedure would be re-run with a fresh candidate. The European Council would have to take account of the results of the European Parliament elections (e.g. as to the relative success of different political groupings) when proposing a candidate for election as Commission President.

The Parliament would continue to have the legal right to approve or reject the proposed membership of the Commission, as a body.

The Commission would continue, at all stages, to take decisions by a simple majority of its members. The allocation of portfolios would be a matter for the Commission President, who could also reshuffle the Commissioners' portfolios during its term of office.

The European Court of Justice (ECJ)

The Court of Justice of the European Union, comprising the Court of Justice supported by specialised courts, will continue to be the institution responsible for interpreting and applying EU law.

1. There will continue to be one judge appointed to the Court of Justice from each of the Member States (i.e. currently 27 judges). Under the Treaty, a panel of seven experts will scrutinise candidates for the Court of Justice;

2. Decisions amending the Court's Statute or creating new specialised courts will now be made by QMV and co-decision;

3. The Court will have increased powers to impose fines on Member States for breaches of EU law;

4. There will be somewhat greater scope for actions to be brought before the Court of Justice, even if the applicant is not affected individually, as was a condition up to now;

5. The legal status of the Charter of Fundamental Rights under the Treaty will significantly increase the jurisdiction of the Court.

European Central Bank (ECB)

The ECB is the central bank for Europe's single currency, the euro. The euro is the official currency of the 15 EU Member States, including Ireland, that have introduced the euro since 1999.

The Treaty of Lisbon formalises the position of the ECB by making it an institution of the European Union. The Treaty also gives the ECB wider power to adopt measures concerning international aspects of monetary union.

The European System of Central Banks (ESCB)

The ESCB comprises the ECB and the national central banks of all EU Member States whether or not they have adopted the euro.

The Euro Group, which comprises the Member States of the euro zone, is also given a formal status by the Treaty. The Euro Group can adopt a recommendation on whether a new Member State should join the eurozone.

Other EU Bodies

The Treaty also makes minor changes regarding the EU Court of Auditors, the two main EU advisory bodies – the Economic and Social Committee and the Committee of the Regions – and the European Investment Bank.

EU POWERS AND DECISIONMAKING

The Treaty makes clear that it is the Member States who confer powers (competences) on the EU in order to attain objectives which they have in common. Powers not conferred upon the EU remain with the Member States and the new Treaty strengthens controls on actions which could better be taken at the level of the Member States.

Exclusive competence
The EU has exclusive competence in some areas (i.e. only the EU may legislate; Member States can only do so if empowered by the EU or to implement EU legislation). The EU has exclusive competence for:

- customs union;
- competition rules necessary for the internal market
- monetary policy (for the Member States whose currency is the euro);
- conservation under the common fisheries policy;
- common commercial policy;
- conclusion of certain international agreements.

Shared competence
The EU will have shared competence with the Member States in a wide range of other areas. Shared competence means that the Member States can take action if the EU does not act. If the EU takes action which is limited to some particular elements of the area (e.g. energy policy), Member States are free to take action on other elements of that area. The following are the principal areas of competence:

- internal market;
- social policy, for the aspects defined in this Treaty;
- economic, social and territorial cohesion;
- agriculture and fisheries, excluding the conservation of marine biological resources;
- environment;
- consumer protection;
- transport;
- trans-European networks;
- energy;
- area of freedom, security and justice;
- common safety concerns in public health matters, for the aspects defined in this Treaty.

The EU and the Member States will each have competence to carry out activities and implement programmes in the areas of research, technological development and space.

In the areas of development cooperation and humanitarian aid, the Union will have competence to carry out activities but this does not prevent Member States from also having programmes in these fields.

The EU will have a specific coordinating role on Member States' actions for:

- economic policies;
- employment policies;
- social policies.

Supporting Role

In addition to areas where the EU has exclusive or shared competence, the EU will have competence to support, coordinate or supplement the actions of the Member States in the areas of:

- protection and improvement of human health;
- industry;
- culture;
- tourism;
- education, vocational training, youth and sport;
- civil protection;
- administrative cooperation.

New legal bases

The EU can only take action if it has a legal base in the Treaty. The Treaty of Lisbon provides new legal bases which would allow the EU to take action on:

- public health (such as disease prevention), in response to wider concerns affecting the safety of the general public;
- energy security;
- dealing with natural or man-made disasters;
- sport;
- space policy.

DECISIONMAKING

The general rule will be that European legislation will be decided by the Council and the European Parliament interacting on an equal footing, on the basis of proposals made by the Commission. In the great majority of areas, only the Commission could put forward proposals. These arrangements are termed, in the new Treaty, the Ordinary Legislative Procedure.

There are a small number of exceptions. Foreign policy is one such area where separate, specific decisionmaking procedures will apply.

Another important exception relates to

- judicial cooperation in criminal matters;
- police cooperation.

In these areas, legislative proposals can be made by Member States numbering at least one-quarter of the total (currently, seven Member States).

The new Treaty changes the procedures under which the EU budget will be adopted by the European Parliament and the Council.

Principles that EU law-making must respect

The new Treaty and protocols attached to it significantly strengthen certain principles first set down in earlier treaties and streamline how decisions would be made.

The use of EU powers is governed by the principles of subsidiarity and proportionality. The Treaty elaborates on these principles and adds control mechanisms.

Under the principle of subsidiarity, the EU acts only where its objectives could not be sufficiently achieved by the Member States, whether at central, regional or local level, but could be better achieved at EU level.

Clearly, this principle relates to cases where either the EU or the Member States could act – and not to areas where the EU has exclusive powers.

Under the principle of proportionality, the type and substance of EU action should not go any further than what is necessary to achieve the aims of the treaties, e.g. a regulation should not be proposed where a recommendation would suffice: if a regulation is needed, it should only cover what is strictly necessary. A legally binding protocol lays down how these principles are to be applied in detail. Any disputes over the application of the principles would be decided by the European Court of Justice.

Democratic principles

The Treaty of Lisbon introduces new provisions regarding citizenship and representative democracy.

Every national of a Member State is also a citizen of the EU. This EU citizenship is additional to – not a replacement of - national citizenship. Citizens are directly represented in the European Parliament while the Member States are represented in the European Council and in the Council by their governments which are in turn democratically accountable either to their National Parliaments, or to their citizens.

National Parliaments are given new functions in certain areas, particularly to ensure respect for "subsidiarity" and in future revisions of the Treaties.

National Parliaments will be given at least eight weeks in which to consider any proposed EU legislation before it is put to the Council. National Parliaments will receive key documents such as Council agendas, Commission communications and the Commission's legislative programme.

National Parliaments can vote to issue a 'reasoned opinion' on whether or not a Commission proposal respects the principle of subsidiarity. Each national Parliament has two votes in this system (the Dáil and the Seanad will each have one vote). If at least one-third (currently 18) of such votes are issued, the Commission's draft must be reviewed. However the Commission is not obliged to amend or reject the proposal. In the case of proposals in the areas of judicial co-operation in criminal matters and police co-operation, the threshold is one-quarter of the votes (currently, 14).

If it chooses to maintain the proposal, the Commission will have to justify, in a reasoned opinion, why it considers that the proposal complies with the principle of subsidiarity.

If a majority of national parliaments oppose a Commission proposal as a breach of subsidiarity, and the Council or the European Parliament agree with them, then the proposal can be struck down. These two levels of control, known as 'yellow cards' and 'orange cards', are set out in a special Protocol.

As a last resort, national parliaments or Member State governments or, in cases relevant to its functions, the Committee of the Regions, would have the power to refer their concerns about any breach of subsidiarity to the European Court of Justice, for a binding ruling.

Provision is also made for a "Citizens' Initiative" where at least one million citizens from a number of Member States can invite the Commission to submit a proposal on any matter where citizens want legislation to implement the Treaties. The Commission is obliged to consider the proposal.

Changes In Decisionmaking

Under the Treaty, there will be significant changes in how EU institutions make decisions.

The European Parliament is given co-decision powers in many additional areas. The voting system in the Council would change from unanimity to QMV in further areas. A list of these areas is attached to this Summary Guide.

The Treaty also creates special procedures – detailed below - which would extend QMV and/or co-decision under the Treaty if the European Council so decides unanimously.

Until 2014, the definition of QMV in the Treaty of Nice would continue to apply. From 1 November 2014, a new definition of QMV would come into operation. From then on, a qualified majority, also known as "double majority", would be defined as 55 per cent of the members of the EU comprising at least 15 Member States representing 65 per cent of the population of the EU. On the other hand, a proposal can only be blocked if it is opposed by at least four Member States (a blocking minority).

Currently, 255 votes are required out of a total of 345 votes (of which Ireland has 7 votes). The new "double-majority", if applied now, would require support by

- 15 out of 27 Member States;
- Member States representing a total population of 322 million, out of an EU total of 495 million (Ireland currently has approx. 0.85 per cent of the total EU population).

For a transitional period (from 1 November 2014 to 31 March 2017), a Member State may request application of the current weighted voting system, instead of the double-majority system.

Under the new system, a group of states that cannot form a blocking minority can temporarily suspend a decision of the Council if the group represents at least 75 per cent of the number of Member States or 75 per cent of the population needed to block a proposal. In that event, the Council will continue to discuss the proposal for a "reasonable time".

From 1 April 2017, the 75 per cent threshold will be lowered to 55 per cent and this can be reduced to a simple majority by a decision of the European Council (i.e. by unanimity).

When not acting on a proposal from the Commission or the Minister for Foreign Affairs, a qualified majority would be defined as 72 per cent of the Members of the EU representing 65 per cent of the population of its Member States

The need for a unanimous vote will remain in almost 60 cases.

ENHANCED COOPERATION

'Enhanced co-operation' is a set of arrangements which could have effect where some Member States, but not all, want to co-operate more closely in a particular area.

Enhanced co-operation, which currently requires one-third of Member States, will require at least nine Member States under the new Treaty and

- would have to be open, then and later, to all Member States;
- where it related to internal EU matters, external economic relations and humanitarian aid, would have to get the backing of the Commission, be approved by the Council and be accepted by the European Parliament;
- where it related to common foreign and security policy, would have to be approved by the Council acting unanimously;
- could only be a last resort (where it is clear that the objectives in view could not be achieved by the EU as a whole within a reasonable timeframe);
- cannot be used with respect to areas of exclusive competence.

It would also have to

- avoid undermining the single market or regional policy in the EU;
- not be a barrier to, or lead to discrimination in trade between, Member States;
- not distort competition.

Under the new Treaty, the previous ban on enhanced co-operation being used in the security and defence area no longer applies.

COMMON FOREIGN AND SECURITY POLICY (CFSP)

The Common Foreign and Security Policy (CFSP), which covers all aspects of foreign and security policy, is based on a separate chapter of the Treaty of European Union. CFSP currently forms a separate part of the EU's so-called "Second Pillar", which operates largely through intergovernmental decisionmaking. The new Treaty would abolish this separate "Pillar" ending its inter-governmental character but CFSP would have special decisionmaking rules. The EU's action in the wider world will be guided by a set of principles which include democracy, the rule of law and respect for the UN Charter.

Decisions in regard to the Common Foreign and Security Policy would, in general, continue to be made by unanimity. However, there would be two exceptions. Firstly, the Treaty specifically provides for the possibility of QMV where a particular decision relates to a policy previously decided at summit level or, alternatively, to details of implementation. But, even in these cases, a Member State could, for vital and stated reasons of national policy, veto any resort to decision by QMV.

Secondly, there is a general clause, under which the European Council could decide unanimously to transfer decisions from unanimity to the QMV category in any Common Foreign and Security Policy domain, other than military and defence aspects (detailed below).

Common Security and Defence Policy (CSDP)

The Common Foreign and Security Policy would enable the EU to draw on civil and military resources provided by the Member States to take part in missions outside its borders. These would be

- joint disarmament operations;
- humanitarian and rescue tasks;
- military advice and assistance tasks;
- conflict prevention;
- peace-keeping;
- tasks of combat forces in crisis management (including peacemaking and post-conflict stabilisation);

- to strengthen international security, in line with the principles of the United Nations Charter.

Such missions would only be authorised by a unanimous vote of the Council on a proposal from the High Representative of the Union for Foreign Affairs and Security Policy or a Member State.

The Treaty will, however, allow for those Member States with bigger military capabilities to commit to taking part together in the most demanding missions within the external tasks listed above.

This will be called **"Structured Co-operation"**.

Only Ministers of those Member States taking part in this arrangement would be allowed to debate and vote in the Council on any action proposed under this pact.

Member States would be bound to support the EU's Common Foreign and Security Policy and not to impede its implementation. They would also have to consult each other or major foreign and security policy issues, especially before undertaking any actions or commitments that could affect the common interests of the EU.

In regard to defence within EU borders, the new Treaty also explicitly states that the security and defence policy will include the progressive framing of a common defence policy and that this "will lead to a common defence" when the European Council unanimously so decides.

Any such decision would have to be ratified constitutionally – which, should Ireland wish to participate in such a common defence, would require a 'yes' in a referendum. The Treaty does not amend the "Seville Declaration" on Irish neutrality made at the European Council in 2002.

Any policy in this area would respect the neutrality of Member States like Ireland would respect the obligations of other Member States which are part of NATO and fit in with the security and defence policy established in that framework.

Pending any European Council decision to move to a

common defence against external aggression, the Treaty provides for "Closer co-operation" between willing Member States on mutual defence – this would oblige those States to go to the aid of a fellow EU country which was a participant in such co-operation and came under armed aggression.

The European Defence Agency was established by the Council of Ministers in July 2004 with the aim of supporting the Member States and the Council "in their efforts to improve European defence capabilities in the field of crisis management and to sustain the European Security and Defence Policy as it stands now and develops in the future". It is open to all Member States "wishing to be part of it" – all but Denmark have already done so.

The new Treaty introduces a new area of solidarity that would be expected of all EU members. The Solidarity Clause says that the EU and its Member States would act jointly in a spirit of solidarity if a Member State were the victim of a terrorist attack or a natural or man-made disaster.

The EU would mobilise all its resources, civil and military, to:

- prevent the terrorist threat in the territory of the Member States;
- protect democratic institutions and the civilian population from any terrorist attack;
- assist a Member State in its territory at the request of its political authorities if a terrorist attack happened;
- assist a Member State in its territory at the request of its political authorities in the event of a disaster.

Precise arrangements for putting this clause into effect would be settled unanimously by the Council, on the basis of a joint proposal by the Commission and the High Representative of the Union for Foreign Affairs and Security Policy.

The Treaty recognises that Member States may come to each other's assistance in the face of armed aggression, in keeping with the UN Charter.

FREEDOM, SECURITY AND JUSTICE

The European Union defines itself as an area of freedom, security and justice. In a Europe where people move freely across borders, police and judicial cooperation is required to protect people from terrorism and serious crime.

The new Treaty sets out to do this by including provisions that would

- give the EU more powers in the Justice and Home Affairs area;
- enhance the EU's effectiveness in fields where it has already been active – external border control, visas, asylum and immigration, judicial cooperation in criminal matters and police cooperation;
- extend the EU's field of action in the fight against serious cross-border crime, police co-operation, mutual recognition of decisions by courts and judges and the creation of a EU public prosecutor, with functions in defined areas.

The EU would

- ensure the absence of border controls inside the EU;
- frame a common policy, including passing legislative measures on asylum, immigration and control at the EU's outside borders, based on solidarity, financially and otherwise, between Member States and also fairness to the people of countries outside the EU;
- promote and take measures to prevent and fight crime, racism and hatred of foreigners and for co-operation between police forces, prosecutors, courts and judges; and also by mutual recognition of judgments in criminal matters and, if needed, bringing Member States' criminal laws closer together;
- promote access to justice, especially by mutual recognition of decisions in Member States in civil law matters.

Under the existing treaties, the EU can already act in the areas of police co-operation and judicial co-operation on criminal matters, but using inter-governmental co-operation methods, with a limited role of the Parliament and Court of Justice, rather than the normal 'Community method'.

Under the new Treaty, the handling of these areas would be more in line with normal EU procedures, where the Commission makes proposals, the European Parliament and Council co-legislate on an equal footing (including qualified majority voting in the Council). The legislation adopted will be subject to greater scrutiny by the Court of Justice. One special feature: a quarter of Member States could propose a measure, in the same way as the Commission.

Ireland and the UK have special opt-out/ opt-in arrangements in this field (details below).

As regards judicial co-operation in criminal matters, the Council could set down minimum standards for the definition of offences and for penalties in regard to listed serious and cross-border offences – organised crime, terrorism, trafficking in human beings, sexual exploitation of women and children, drugs and arms trafficking, money laundering, counterfeiting, computer crime and corruption.

Under the proposals, the EU could also decide on criminal procedure, setting down minimum rules with regard to the rights of individuals in such procedure and the rights of victims – but adoption of such rules would not prevent Member States from maintaining or introducing a higher standard of protection for the rights of individuals.

Where a Member State considers that proposed legislation in this area would affect fundamental aspects of its criminal justice system, it may request that the proposal be referred to the European Council where consensus will be required for the proposal to proceed. If there is disagreement, Member States supporting the proposal can proceed by the "enhanced cooperation" mechanism. (A similar 'emergency brake' mechanism will apply to proposals on social security for migrant workers.)

The mechanisms for judicial co-operation in this field, such as Eurojust, would be strengthened but also, for the first time, made subject to evaluation by the European Parliament and national parliaments. At some time in the future, the Council could decide, by unanimous vote, to set up a European Public Prosecutor's Office to track down and prosecute the perpetrators of, and accomplices in crimes affecting the financial interests of the EU, with the option of extending its powers to include serious crime having cross-border dimensions.

The Treaty provides, for the first time, that Europol, too, would be subject to evaluation by the European Parliament and national parliaments.

Ireland's Opt-out/Opt-In

The provisions of the new Treaty in the areas of criminal law and police cooperation are based on the proposals in the European Constitution which were agreed under the Irish Presidency. However, during the negotiations leading to the Treaty of Lisbon, the UK decided to exercise an opt-out in this area which created important implications for Ireland's position, particularly as Ireland and Britain both have common law systems which are quite distinct from other European legal systems. In a situation where the UK has opted-out, Ireland would be acting alone in seeking to shape proposals to take account of our legal practice and tradition. The opt-out arrangement includes a provision which allows Ireland (and the UK) to opt into future measures on a case-by-case basis. In a separate Declaration on these arrangements, Ireland has indicated its intention to opt-in to all such measures to the maximum extent it deems possible. Ireland also declared its intention to review the operation of these arrangements within three years (i.e. as early as 1 January 2012).

THE CHARTER OF FUNDAMENTAL RIGHTS

The European Union Charter of Fundamental Rights sets out the civil, political, economic and social rights recognised by the EU. The text of the Charter was the outcome of a special Convention which met between 1999 – 2000 and comprised representatives of Member States' Governments, National Parliaments, the European Parliament and the Commission.

The Charter gives the European Court of Justice a new reference point on human rights but it does not add the competences of the Court.

The text of the Charter was unanimously approved by the European Council in October 2000 and subsequently by the European Parliament and the Commission. The Charter was signed and proclaimed on behalf of all three institutions at the European Council in Nice (December 2000). It has been revised to clarify its scope and limits and was re-proclaimed by the EU institutions on 12 December 2007. The revised version of the Charter will take effect on the same day that the new Treaty will enter into force.

The Treaty, while not incorporating the text of the Charter, gives the Charter the same legal value as the main Treaties.

Nothing in the Charter is to be interpreted as restricting or adversely affecting human rights, as recognised by, for example, the Member States' constitutions.

The content of the Charter is broader than that of the 1950 European Convention for the Protection of Human Rights and Fundamental Freedoms (EHCR). It draws on the previous European Social Charters worked out by both the EU and the Council of Europe. While the ECHR is limited to civil and political rights, the Charter of Fundamental Rights covers other areas.

The Charter contains a preamble and 54 Articles, grouped in following chapters:

Chapter I: Dignity, which includes:

- human dignity;
- the right to life;
- the right to the integrity of the person;
- prohibition of torture and inhuman or degrading treatment or punishment;
- prohibition of slavery and forced labour.

Chapter II: Freedoms, which include:

- the right to liberty and security;
- respect for private and family life, protection of personal data;
- the right to marry and found a family;
- freedom of thought, conscience and religion;
- freedom of expression and information;
- freedom of assembly and association;
- freedom of the arts and sciences;
- the right to education;
- freedom to choose an occupation and the right to engage in work, freedom to conduct a business;
- the right to property;
- the right to asylum, and protection in the event of removal, expulsion or extradition.

Chapter III: Equality, which includes:

- equality before the law;
- non-discrimination;
- cultural, religious and linguistic diversity;
- equality between men and women;
- the rights of the child;
- the rights of the elderly;
- integration of persons with disabilities.

Chapter IV: Solidarity, which includes:

- workers' right to information and consultation within the undertaking;
- the right of collective bargaining and action;

- the right of access to placement services;
- protection in the event of unjustified dismissal;
- fair and just working conditions;
- prohibition of child labour and protection of young people at work;
- protection regarding the family and professional life;
- social security and social assistance;
- health care;
- access to services of general economic interest;
- environmental protection;
- consumer protection.

Chapter V: Citizens' Rights, which include:

- the right to vote and stand as a candidate at elections to the European Parliament;
- the right to vote and stand as a candidate at municipal elections;
- the right to good administration;
- the right of access to documents;
- Right of reference to the EU Ombudsman;
- the right to petition the European Parliament;
- Freedom of movement and residence;
- diplomatic and consular protection.

Chapter VI: Justice, which includes:

- the right to an effective remedy and a fair trial;
- the presumption of innocence and the right of defence;
- principles of legality and proportionality of criminal offences and penalties, the right not to be tried or punished twice in criminal proceedings for the same criminal offence.

Chapter VII: General provisions

In general, the rights referred to apply to everyone. However, the Charter also refers to categories of persons with special needs (children, the elderly, people with a disability). Chapter V also deals with the specific situation of European citizens,

referring to certain rights already mentioned in the treaties (freedom of movement and residence, the right to vote, the right to petition) and introducing the right to good administration.

Recognising the changes that have occurred in society, the Charter includes not only the traditional rights (right to life, freedom of expression, right to an effective remedy), but also rights that were not included in the Council of Europe Convention of 1950 (data protection, bioethics). Using more modern language, in line with certain national legislation, it also recognises ways of founding a family other than by marriage and no longer refers to marriage between men and women, but simply marriage, although recognising that this is a matter for each Member State.

The general provisions serve to establish links between the Charter and the European Convention on Human Rights and to determine the scope of the Charter. The Charter applies to the European institutions, subject to the principle of subsidiarity, and may under no circumstances extend the powers and tasks conferred on them by the treaties. The principles of the Charter also apply to the Member States (to central, regional and local authorities) when they are implementing Union law.

The EU will also accede to the European Convention on Human Rights, subject to the unanimous approval of the Council and the completion of domestic ratification procedures by the Member States.

The rights under the Charter, as now incorporated, apply to every person in the EU except where it is stated that they are 'citizens rights' and thus in principle apply only to those who are EU citizens.

CHANGES IN ECONOMIC GOVERNANCE FIELD

The Treaty proposes to strengthen the powers given to the European Commission where Member States have excessive budget deficits. In the future, the Council would only be able to diverge from a Commission proposal concerning the existence of an excessive deficit, by unanimous vote, as opposed to the present situation where the Commission makes a recommendation which Finance Ministers do not have to accept.

The proposals also include a new set of articles specific to Member States which are part of the Euro area. A related protocol is annexed to the Treaty of Lisbon, under which

- provision is proposed for specific economic policy guidelines for those Member States;
- provision is made for the Eurozone Ministers to settle common positions on matters arising in international financial institutions and conferences that are relevant to the euro and its management;
- provision is made whereby the informal grouping of Eurozone Finance Ministers would have an elected President for a two and a half year period, replacing the rotation system that operated up to now.

A Protocol is added to the Treaty on "Services of General Interest" which indicates the shared values regarding services of general economic interest and makes clear that the competence of Member States is not affected by the Treaty in regard to non-economic services of general interest.

PROCEDURE FOR FUTURE AMENDMENTS

The Treaty of Lisbon sets out two procedures for amending the EU Treaties, the "Ordinary Revision Procedure" which is equivalent to the traditional procedures, and the "Simplified Revision Procedures" which are limited in scope.

The "Ordinary Revision Procedure"

The decision as to whether to examine any proposed amendments would be taken by the European Council, by a simple majority, after consulting the European Parliament.

If the European Council says "no", that would be the end for the proposed amendment. If its answer were "yes", its President would have to convene a Convention, with membership as inclusive as in the Convention on the Future of Europe (described above).

However, if they decided, again by a simple majority, that the proposed amendments were not important enough to warrant calling a Convention, it would be for an IGC to do this work. Where a Convention was held, it would adopt a consensus recommendation on the proposed amendments. This would then be considered by an IGC, which would, as now, have to reach a unanimous decision. Before any amendments could enter into force, they would have to be ratified by all Member States in accordance with their constitutional requirements.

If, two years after the signing of any such treaty, at least four-fifths of Member States had ratified that treaty but one or more others had met difficulties in doing so, the matter would have to be referred to the European Council, to consider what to do.

Simplified Revision Procedures

The Simplified Revision Procedures relate to specific, limited aspects of the Treaties. Amendments to Part III of the TFEU (EU Policies and Internal Actions) could be decided by the European Council but this decision would have to be approved by all the Member States in accordance with their constitutional procedures (e.g. parliamentary ratification, referendum).

Except for military and defence issues, the European Council would also be able to allow

(a) qualified majority voting where unanimity is required, and

(b) the "ordinary legislative procedure" where special procedures apply (giving co-decision powers to the European Parliament).

However, any national parliament could block such a change within six months. This clause is known as the "general passerelle", from the French word meaning "footbridge".

In addition, there are some specific "passerelle" clauses – where the European Council, acting unanimously, could introduce qualified majority voting in specific areas where unanimity is currently required.

CLAUSES OF GENERAL APPLICATION

A short series of articles seeks to ensure that wider EU objectives – gender equality, opposition to discrimination on multiple grounds, protection of the environment, the fight against social exclusion, consumer protection, reduction of regional disparities, widespread access to services of general economic interest – are taken fully into account when defining and implementing each specific policy of the EU.

Provision is made for the adoption of legislative measures, if and as necessary, to combat discrimination on any of a range of grounds; to facilitate the exercise of the right to move and reside freely within the EU; and to fix the detailed arrangements for the exercise of the rights of European citizens to vote, where they live, in European Parliament and local elections.

An article clarifies in which languages citizens have a right to address, and get a reply from, the EU institutions and advisory bodies – these include the Irish language.

ADOPTION, RATIFICATION AND ENTRY INTO FORCE OF THE TREATY OF LISBON (EU REFORM TREATY)

As with previous EU Treaties, the new Treaty can only enter into force if it is ratified by all 27 Member States in accordance with the constitutional procedures of each Member State. The Treaty could come into effect on 1 January 2009 if all Member States have ratified it by that date.

The Treaty is valid in all the EU's official languages, including the Irish language.

GLOSSARY OF TREATY TERMS

Explanatory Note

The terms explained in this glossary are, in general, ones that occur in the Treaty of Lisbon (EU Reform Treaty), where the meaning may not be clear to the ordinary person who is not an expert on European affairs and where it is not explained fully in the text of the summary. A small number of other words or phrases which often arise in discussions about the matters dealt with in the Treaty are also included.

Accountability

The capacity or duty to account in an open, transparent manner for actions taken, or not taken, whether by an individual or an institution.

Appropriations

In the EU context, this is a term relating to the budget and refers to amounts of money to be committed to be spent at some time in the next short period of years (commitment appropriations) or actually to be spent in the current or forthcoming financial year (expenditure appropriations).

(To) Approximate (National Laws)

This means to bring about a situation where the law applying in certain areas of life in the different Member States is more closely similar but not necessarily exactly the same.

Charter of Fundamental Rights

This Charter, adopted by an earlier Convention in October 2000, sets out in a single text, for the first time in the European Union's history, civil, political, economic and social rights and freedoms of European citizens and all persons resident in the EU. Before its adoption, these rights were laid down in a variety of national, European and international sources. The Charter had been incorporated into the European Constitution but it will not form part of the text of the new Treaty, although it will be given the same legal status as treaties. It would apply to the EU's Institutions and to the Member States' governments only when they were implementing EU law.

Co-decision

The procedure through which the Council and the European Parliament enact most EU legislation. Under the new Treaty, it will form part of the Ordinary Legislative Procedure.

Common Foreign and Security Policy (CFSP)

Following on from earlier efforts, since the early 1970s, at cooperation in the area of foreign policy, the Common Foreign and Security Policy was established as the "second pillar" in the Maastricht Treaty (1992) and developed under the Amsterdam Treaty (1997) and the Treaty of Nice (2001). The common policy exists in parallel to the separate foreign and security policies of the EU Member States. The new Treaty contains extensive provisions on Common Foreign and Security Policy which are summarised above.

Community Method (Community Way)

The "Community method" refers to the unique institutional procedures brought into being by the Treaty of Rome, defining relations between sovereign states of unequal size who agree to pool sovereignty. The Community method involves an institutional structure where the European Commission alone has the right to propose European legislation and where decisions are made in an interaction between the Council and the European Parliament. These decisions are open to challenge before the European Court of Justice.

Principle of Conferral

The principle of conferral means that the EU does not have general competences in its own right, but only those that are specifically conferred upon it by the Member States in the founding treaties and their subsequent modifications. The EU can only act on the basis of a provision of the treaties that authorises it to do so. In treaty terms, competence means the legal capacity or ability to legislate or to take other action.

Conferred Powers

This refers to the principle whereby the EU has only the powers conferred on its institutions by the treaties. Powers not conferred remain with the Member States.

Convergence

Becoming more alike or closer together in terms of various characteristics or capabilities.

Council of Europe

The Council of Europe is an intergovernmental organisation, set up in 1948, which includes in its aims the protection of

NATIONAL FORUM ON EUROPE

FÓRAM NÁISIÚNTA UM AN EORAIP

human rights and the promotion and awareness of Europe's cultural identity and diversity. It has a wider membership than the EU. Though all Member States of the EU are also members of the Council of Europe, the latter is a distinct organisation in its own right.

Council of Ministers / Council

The Council of Ministers (formally named simply the Council) is the EU institution in which the governments of the Member States are represented. The Council consists of one representative of each Member State at Ministerial level. The Council meets in a whole range of formations, mainly sectoral (e.g. the Ministers for Agriculture when the Council takes decisions on the Common Agricultural Policy). The President (or chair) of the Council is the Minister of the Member State currently holding the EU Presidency. Up to now, this was for a six-month term according to an agreed and equal rotation. The Treaty of Lisbon contains some changes in regard to the Council of Ministers, which are summarised in this document.

Digressively Proportional

This refers to a system of representation of EU Member States in the European Parliament, whereby the number of seats a country has is broadly proportional to the size of its population but with the ratio between the number of seats and the population size being progressively more favourable the smaller the size of a country's population.

Delegated Act

Under the proposals in the new Treaty, where there are non-essential elements to a legislative measure, these laws may delegate to the European Commission the power to enact detailed measures to supplement or amend these elements. The objective, content, scope and duration of these delegations has to be defined in the original legislative measure. The Council of Ministers and the European Parliament are to supervise the use of this power and may also revoke any such delegation.

Direct Universal Suffrage

Election directly under a system where all persons of voting age are eligible to vote.

Economic, Social and Territorial Cohesion

This means balanced and sustainable development, reducing economic, social and infrastructural inequalities between regions and countries and promoting equal opportunities for all individuals. In practical terms, the EU seeks to achieve these aims by means of a variety of financing operations, principally through the Structural Funds.

Enhanced Cooperation

Enhanced cooperation is the term used to describe a specific EU provision, first introduced in the Treaty of Amsterdam (1997), which allows groups of Member States fewer than the entire membership of the EU to avail of the institutions of the EU in order to undertake closer co-operation between themselves. The Nice Treaty sets out in a consolidated format the pre-conditions for authorisation of enhanced cooperation. The Treaty of Lisbon contains some changes in regard to what has applied up to now, as regards Enhanced Co-operation. These are summarised in this document.

Euratom

The European Atomic Energy Community was created in 1958 by the European Atomic Energy Treaty. The Euratom Treaty is not amended by the Treaty of Lisbon and Euratom will continue to operate under the EU's institutional framework. A declaration by five Member States, including Ireland, notes that the main provisions of the Euratom Treaty, which have never been amended, need to be brought up to date as soon as possible by an intergovernmental conference to revise the Treaty.

Euro

The euro is the European Union's single currency which has been adopted to date by 15 Member States (Austria, Belgium, Cyprus, Finland, France, Germany, Greece, Ireland, Italy, Luxembourg, Malta, the Netherlands, Portugal, Slovenia, Spain), an area unofficially known as the "Eurozone".

European Defence Agency

The European Defence Agency was established in 2004 to support the Member States and the Council in their effort to improve European defence capabilities in the field of crisis management, to monitor the capability commitments of Member States, and to promote harmonisation of procurement and support defence technology research.

European Commission

The European Commission is one of the EU institutions. It was created as an independent body to represent the European interest common to all Member States. Currently, the 27 members of the Commission are drawn from each of the EU countries, but they each swear an oath of independence, distancing themselves from partisan influence from any source. The Commission is the driving force in the legislative process, proposing the legislation on which the European Parliament and the Council of Ministers make decisions. The new Treaty contains changes in regard to the Commission. These are summarised in this document.

European Council

The European Council is the term used to describe the institution within which the Heads of State or Government of the EU Member States meet regularly. It meets at least twice a year – more recently, about four times – and the President of the European Commission attends as a full member. Its functions are to give the EU the impetus it needs in order to develop and to define general policy guidelines and priorities. The new Treaty contains changes in regard to the European Council. These are summarised in this document.

European Convention on Human Rights (ECHR)

The European Convention on Human Rights and Fundamental Freedoms, signed in 1950 under the aegis of the Council of Europe, sets out a list of human rights, which the participating countries guarantee to respect and uphold. The Convention established, for the first time, a system of international protection for human rights offering individuals the possibility of applying to a dedicated international court – the European Court of Human Rights – for the enforcement of their rights. All Member States of the EU have ratified the Convention. The new Treaty envisages that the EU, as such, would seek to join the Convention.

European Court of Auditors

The Court of Auditors is an institution that acts like the auditors of a business or other organisation. It monitors the

EU's accounts, examining the legality and regularity of the revenue and expenditure in the budget and ensuring sound financial management.

Court of Justice of the European Union

This is the institution responsible for interpreting and enforcing EU law. The Court has one judge from each Member State. It has jurisdiction in disputes between Member States, between the EU and its Member States and between institutions and private individuals and the EU about matters that fall within the remit of the EU or are regulated by EU legislation or decisions.

Eurojust

The European Judicial Co-operation Unit. A body of national prosecutors, magistrates or police officers from the Member States, established in 2002 under the Treaty of Nice to coordinate the fight against crime. The Treaty of Lisbon contains some changes in respect of Eurojust and its work which are summarised in this document.

Europol

European Police Office, established under an agreement reached in 1995 and which entered into force on 1 October 1998, but only became fully operational on 1 July 1999. Europol's headquarters are in The Hague and it coordinates police co-operation throughout the EU in particular, agreed areas, for example in the areas of drug trafficking, clandestine immigration networks, trafficking in stolen vehicles, trafficking in human beings (including child pornography), counterfeiting currency and falsification of other means of payment, trafficking in radioactive and nuclear substances, terrorism and money-laundering. The Treaty contains some changes in respect of Europol and its work which are summarised in this document.

European Ombudsman

The office of the European Ombudsman is empowered to receive and investigate complaints from any citizen of the EU or any natural or legal person residing in a Member State concerning instances of alleged bad or unfair administration in the activities of the EU institutions or bodies and to follow up and report on the outcomes.

European Parliament

The European Parliament is the EU institution that represents the citizens of the Member States. It currently consists of 732 members directly elected by the electorates in constituencies in the 25 Member States. In many areas, the Parliament has co-decision powers in legislating with the Council. The Parliament and the Council of Ministers jointly constitute the budgetary authority. The Treaty contains a number of changes affecting the make-up and powers of the Parliament. These changes are summarised in this document.

European Security and Defence Policy (ESDP)

Established in 1999 at the Cologne European Council, the ESDP aims to allow the EU to develop its civilian and military capacities for crisis management and conflict prevention at international level, thus helping to maintain peace and international security, in accordance with the United Nations Charter. It will be renamed the Common Security and Defence Policy under the Treaty of Lisbon.

Flexibility Clause

The flexibility clause within the new Treaty, the antecedents of which go back to the Treaty of Rome, allows flexible adjustments of EU competence within the defined remit of the EU. The existing clause can only be used in connection with the common market. The new clause will allow flexibility in all areas of the EU.

Freedom of Establishment

Every EU citizen, through freedom of establishment, is allowed to set up a business in any EU country in the same way and on the same legal basis as a national of that country.

Geneva Convention

UN rules on asylum dating from 1951. They give every refugee the right to have an application for asylum at least considered by the country in which they apply.

Harmonisation

This means co-ordinating national policies, rules and technical standards so closely that products and services, capital and labour can move freely throughout the EU.

Intergovernmental Conference (IGC)

A conference composed of representatives from each Member State in which amendments to the treaties can be agreed through negotiations.

Languages of the Treaty of Lisbon

This refers to the languages in which the Treaty is to be drawn up, each version being equally authentic, as set out in Article IV-10, the last article of the new Treaty: the list includes the Irish language.

Legal Base

In order for the EU to have power to act in any area, that area must have what is known as a "legal base" in the treaty structure. Any areas where the EU is to have such power must be recognised formally and explicitly in the legal structure of the treaties. The Treaty of Lisbon maintains all areas where there were legal bases previously and creates legal bases in some further, limited areas.

Legitimacy

This is a political concept, relating to whether, or how far, a political system or a set of political arrangements or institutions is regarded as being valid and worthy of acceptance or support by the people who are governed under such arrangements or whose lives are affected by what is done by the institutions.

Lisbon Process or Strategy

Launched at an EU summit in Lisbon, Portugal in 2000, the Lisbon Process or Strategy is a voluntary co-ordination (often referred to as the Open Method of Co-ordination) of a whole range of economic, social and sectoral policies among Member States. It aims to make the EU the most competitive and knowledge-based economy in the world by 2010. (Not to be confused with the Treaty of Lisbon which is the subject of this publication)

Mutual Recognition

Instead of harmonisation i.e. making standards within the EU fully consistent by imposing a common, cross-EU law, the EU often uses the method of "mutual recognition" of standards. This means that a national standard in one country – for example regarding what specifications a product must have – is accepted as being valid in all.

Opt-out:

An option to decline to participate in certain measures or arrangements which would otherwise be obligatory.

Opt-in:

An option to participate in certain measures or arrangements in which the Member State would otherwise not participate.

Official Journal of the European Union

This refers to a daily publication setting out the official acts of the EU, such as the laws it has passed, decisions it has taken, contracts it is offering for tender, jobs for which it wants to recruit etc.

Petersberg Tasks

In the Maastricht Treaty of 1992, the Member States of the EU undertook to enhance co-operation on international affairs through the Common Foreign and Security Policy. The Treaty of Amsterdam, 1997 reflects new priorities of humanitarian, rescue, peacekeeping and crisis management tasks – the Petersberg tasks (called after the venue in Germany where agreement on them was reached) – by incorporating these tasks into the European EU's Common Foreign and Security Policy. The Treaty extends the tasks to cover joint disarmament operations, military advice and post-conflict stabilisation.

Principle of Loyal Cooperation

The principle which commits the EU and its individual Member States to assist each other in carrying out tasks, common or co-ordinated, which flow from the obligations they have assumed and refrain from acting in ways that would block or impede discharge of those tasks.

Proportionality

The principle that EU action must not exceed what is necessary to achieve the objectives of the Treaties.

Protocol

A protocol is a legal text, which is usually added (annexed) to a treaty and which deals in a more detailed way with a certain topic e.g. in the new Treaty there is a protocol on subsidiarity and the role of national parliaments. A protocol to a treaty has the same legal status as the treaty itself when it has been ratified by the Member States.

Qualified Majority Voting (QMV)

QMV is the form of decisionmaking used for most Council of Ministers decisions. Currently, each Member State is assigned a number of votes weighted according to a scale which groups together Member States of similar population size. Under the new Treaty a new system of QMV will apply, based on a "Double Majority" as summarised in this document.

Ratification

In the context of international treaties, this is the process by which each State formally decides, through their own national procedures, that a Treaty, previously signed on their behalf, will be legally binding on them. In the case of EU Treaties, including this latest Treaty, the Treaty will only come into force if and when all Member States have completed the process of ratification.

Reasoned Opinion

The European Commission scrutinises steps taken by each Member State to implement EU law and, if dissatisfied, may issue what is known as a "reasoned opinion" to Member States governments. This is a sort of "early warning system" within which the Commission outlines the measures that will need to be taken in order for the Member State (s) to fully implement the EU law in question. Should these measures not be taken, then the Commission refers the matter to the European Court of Justice.

A second meaning of the term arises in the protocol on applying the principles of proportionality. There, the term refers to an opinion with reasons, put forward by a national parliament (or one of its Houses) that a proposal for a law, made by the Commission, is in breach of the principle of subsidiarity. In this case, a reasoned opinion is part of an "early warning system", to be operated by national parliaments.

Right of Initiative

Reflecting its role as guardian of the treaties and defender of the general interest, the European Commission has been given the "right of initiative" which empowers and requires it to make proposals on the matters contained in the Treaty, either because the Treaty expressly so provides or because the Commission considers it necessary.

Currently, the right of initiative is exclusive to the Commission in all areas except Common Foreign and Security Policy, where Member States also have the right to make proposals and some areas of Justice and Home Affairs where only Member States may make proposals.

The new Treaty contains changes in regard to who has the right of initiative in different areas. These are summarised in this document.

Services of General Interest

This is an expression in the treaties to describe telecommunications, water, postal, transport services and other infrastructure in the Member States, as well as education, health, that are widely regarded as basic necessities for a satisfactory life under modern conditions in Europe.

Seville Declaration

Solemn declarations by the Irish Government and the European Council in 2002 relating to Ireland's participation in the Common Security and Defence Policy.

Social Market Economy

This refers to the type of economic model that has characterised the countries in the EU since reconstruction after the Second World War, in which the economy is primarily based on the competitive operation of the market but with significant regulation in the public interest and in addition, in most cases, a significant consultative role for the social partners in the management of the economy and, in some countries, also at firm? level.

Solidarity Clause

A clause contained in the Treaty committing the EU and its Member States to aid another Member State(s) if that Member State(s) is/are the victim of either a terrorist attack or natural or man-made disaster.

Special Legislative Procedure

A number of areas outlined in the Treaty lie outside the remit of the Ordinary Legislative Procedure described above and fall under what is described as a "Special Legislative Procedure". Decisionmaking procedures vary and may allow for a dominant role for either the Council of Ministers or the

European Parliament. In some cases, proposals may come from sources other than the Commission. Unanimity is also allowed for in some cases.

Stability and Growth Pact

An agreement introduced in the lead-up to monetary EU, the aim of the Stability and Growth Pact is to ensure that the Member States continued their budgetary discipline efforts once the single currency was introduced. The pact details technical arrangements on surveillance of budgetary positions as well as co-ordination of economic policies and implementation of an excessive deficit procedure, allowing the Council to penalise any participating Member State which fails to take appropriate measures to end an excessive budget deficit. In the medium term, the Member States have undertaken to pursue the objective of a balanced or nearly balanced budget.

Subsidiarity

The principle that the European EU does not take action (in areas of shared competence) unless it is more effective than action taken at national, regional or local level.

Supranational

Transcending national limits or boundaries. In the context of the EU, the term usually refers to the institutions that exist to pursue the common EU interests, shared by the Member States. It also refers to the discharge of functions and exercise of powers by those institutions, transcending national boundaries, in the domains where the Member States, in the treaties, have conferred those functions and powers on them. The supranational approach is often contrasted with the intergovernmental approach that involves keeping supranational institutions, and their role, to a minimum.

Sustainable Development

A form of economic growth, which is based on the most economical use of resources, particularly those that are scarce and which is thus more likely to satisfy society's needs over the long term, rather than using the resources rapidly in the short term. The concept is founded on the assumption that development, while meeting today's needs or tomorrow's, must do so without jeopardising the prospects of future generations.

Transparency

Making it possible to see clearly and to follow from outside the way in which decisions are reached.

Unanimity

The requirement for all Member States to agree on a proposal before it can be adopted.

Veto

The power to block a proposal.

LIST OF THE ARTICLES COMING UNDER QUALIFIED MAJORITY VOTING

The Lisbon Reform Treaty extends qualified majority voting (QMV) to many new areas and will change the system of QMV from 2014 to a "double majority". While some new areas of QMV are technical or minor, others have major significance. The following summary list shows the main areas which will be subject to QMV and highlights new areas subject to QMV and the most notable changes from unanimity to QMV. Sensitive areas such as taxation, social security, and common defence are still governed by unanimity.

AREAS FOR QMV UNDER THE TREATY ON EUROPEAN UNION *(New areas and areas changed to QMV are in bold italics)*
Election of the President of the European Council by the European Council
Adoption of the list of configurations of the Council of Ministers by the European Council
Proposal of a candidate for the post of President of the Commission by the European Council
Appointment of the Commission by the European Council
Appointment of the High Representative by the European Council, with the approval of the President of the Commission
Decision defining an EU action or position on the basis of a decision of the European Council relating to the EU's strategic interests and objectives
Decision defining an EU action or position on a proposal from the High Representative
Decision implementing a decision defining an EU action or proposition in the area of the CFSP

Appointment of a special representative on a proposal of the High Representative
CFSP Procedural questions
CFSP start-up fund on a proposal of the High Representative
Decision defining the European Defence Agency's statute, seat and operational rules
Decisions establishing permanent structured cooperation, suspending or accepting new members
Conclusion of a withdrawal agreement of a Member State after the approval of the European Parliament and on the request of the State concerned

AREAS FOR QMV UNDER THE TREATY ON THE FUNCTIONING OF THE EUROPEAN UNION *(New areas and areas changed to QMV are in bold italics)*
Regulations relating to services of general economic interest
Regulations relating to general principles and limits of the right to access to documents of EU institutions, offices or agencies
Rules relating to the protection of individuals with regard to the processing of personal data
Prohibition of discrimination on grounds of nationality
Basic principles for EU incentive measures to support action taken by the Member States in the fight against discrimination based on sex, racial or ethnic origin, religion or belief, disability, age or sexual orientation, excluding any harmonisation measure
Provisions with a view to facilitating the exercise of the right to move and reside freely within the territory of the EU
Regulations relating to procedures and conditions required for a citizens' initiative

Establishment of common customs tariff duties on a proposal of the Commission
Measures in order to strengthen customs cooperation
Establishment of the common organisation of agricultural markets and others provisions necessary for the pursuit of the objectives of the common agricultural policy and the common fisheries policy.
Directives or regulations setting out the measures required to bring about freedom of movement for workers.
Provisions relating to the aggregation of periods for the right to, and amount of, social benefit for migrant workers (Unanimity retained on provisions regarding payment of benefits to persons resident in the Member States)
Directives relating to the freedom of establishment as regards a particular activity
Exemption of some activities with regard to the measures in the chapter relating to the right of establishment
Directives relating to the coordination of provisions in terms of right of establishment
Directives relating to the mutual recognition of diplomas, certificates and other evidence of formal qualifications
Coordination of national provisions concerning the taking-up and pursuit of activities as self-employed persons
Extension of the provisions relating to service to nationals of a third country who provide services and who are established within the EU
Directives relative to the liberalisation of a specific service
Measures on the movement of capital to and from third countries involving direct investment - including in real estate - establishment, the provision of financial services or the admission of securities to capital markets
Evaluation measures of the implementation of the area of freedom, security and justice after simply informing the European Parliament and national parliaments

Administrative cooperation within the area of freedom, security and justice after consulting the European Parliament
Regulations relating to administrative measures with regard to capital movements and payments (freezing of funds, financial assets or economic gains)
Measures concerning border checks
Measures concerning a common European asylum system
Provisional emergency measures in case of a sudden inflow of refugees after consulting the European Parliament
Measures concerning a common immigration policy
Measures to provide incentives and support for Member States promoting the integration of third-country nationals (not including harmonisation measures)
Measures concerning the judicial cooperation in civil matters having a cross-border dimension
Measures concerning the judicial cooperation in criminal matters
Directives concerning the basic rules for mutual recognition of court judgements
Directives establishing basic rules concerning the definition of criminal offences and sanctions in the areas of serious crime with a cross-border dimension (terrorism, trafficking in human beings and sexual exploitation of women and children, illicit drug and arms trafficking, organised crime)
Money laundering, corruption, counterfeiting of means of payment, computer crime and organised crime)
Directive establishing minimal harmonisation rules with regard to the definition of criminal offences and sanctions in the area concerned

Measures to promote and support the action of Member States in the field of crime prevention excluding any harmonisation measure
Measures concerning the police cooperation (collection and exchange of information, training of staff, common investigative techniques
Regulations concerning Europol's structure, operation, field of action and tasks
Establishment of rules concerning transport
Provisions for sea and air transport.
Competition rules necessary for the functioning of the internal market
Measures relating to the approximation of national provisions concerning the establishment and functioning of the internal market
Directives necessary to eliminate the distortion of competition in a Member State and when the consultation procedure fails
Measures concerning the creation of European intellectual property rights to provide uniform intellectual property rights protection throughout the EU
Regulations concerning detailed rules for the multilateral surveillance procedure within the Stability and Growth Pact
Amendment of some articles of the Statute of the ESCB
Measures necessary for use of the euro after consulting the European Central Bank
Measures to ensure unified representation within international financial institutions and conferences after consulting the ECB
Incentive measures designed to encourage cooperation between Member States and to support their action in the field of employment

Measures designed to encourage cooperation between Member States in the field of social policy
Directives concerning the minimum requirements for gradual implementation in the social field
Implementing decisions relating to the European Social Fund
Incentive measures in the fields of sport
Incentive measures in the cultural field
Measures to support and supplement the Member States in the field of vocational training
Measures designed to meet common safety concerns with regard to public health (standards relating to organs and substances of human origin, blood and blood derivatives; veterinary and phytosanitary fields; standards for medicinal products and devices for medical use)
Incentive measures designed to protect and improve human health (monitoring, early warning of and combating serious cross-border threats to health, measures to protect public health (tobacco, alcohol)), excluding any harmonisation measure
Measures concerning the consumer protection in the context of the completion of the internal market
Guidelines, measures and projects of common interest concerning the establishment and development of trans-European networks in the areas of transport, telecommunications and energy infrastructures
Specific actions outside the Structural Funds
Regulations and general rules applicable to the Structural Funds
Implementing regulations relating to the European Regional Development Fund
Measures necessary for the implementation of the European area of research

Measures necessary to draw up a European Space Policy that may take the form of a European Space Programme

Actions within the European environment policy

General action programmes setting out priority objectives to be attained in the field of environment

Measures relating to energy policy

Measures necessary for the achievement of objectives relating to cooperation between Member States in order to improve the effectiveness of systems for preventing and protecting against natural and manmade disasters, excluding any harmonisation measure

Measures defining the framework for implementing the common commercial policy

Negotiation and conclusion of agreements with one or more third countries or international organisations in the field of commercial policy

Measures necessary for the implementation of development cooperation policy (multiannual cooperation programmes with developing countries, thematic programmes)

Measures necessary for the implementation of economic, financial and technical cooperation measures including assistance, in particular financial assistance, with third countries other than developing countries

Urgent financial assistance measures for developing countries

Measures defining the framework within which the EU's humanitarian aid operations are implemented

Interruption or reduction of economic and financial relations with third countries on a joint proposal of the High Representative

Conclusion of international agreements (except for association agreements or economic, financial and technical cooperation agreements or if the field covered by the agreement requires unanimity)

Implementation of the solidarity clause in the event of a terrorist attack or a disaster (on a joint proposal of the High Representative and the Commission)
Regulations governing political parties at European level
Decision by the European Council on the Presidency of Council configurations (other than that of Foreign Affairs)
Procedural decisions within the Council and adoption of its Rules of Procedure
*Amendment of the provisions of the Court of Justice's Statute (*with some exceptions*)*
Appointment of the president, vice-president and members of the ECB Governing Council by the European Council
Conditions of employment and remuneration of the president and the members of the Court of Auditors
Rules and general principles concerning mechanisms for control by Member States of the Commission's exercise of implementing powers
Regulations concerning the establishment and implementation of the budget, the presentation and audit of accounts
Necessary measures in the fields of the prevention of and fight against fraud affecting the financial interests of the EU after consulting the Court of Auditors
Decision of the Council following a decision to suspend voting rights

COMPARISON WITH THE EUROPEAN CONSTITUTION

1. The "Constitutional characteristics" are abandoned, notably by reverting to the system of an amending Treaty rather than replacing the existing Treaties;

2. Express provisions for EU symbols (flag, anthem, motto, Europe Day) have been dropped;

3. The title of the 'Union Minister of Foreign Affairs' has changed;

4. The Charter of Fundamental Rights is not part of the Treaty although it is legally binding;

5. The clauses on primacy of EU law have been dropped;

6. The objectives of the EU do not include a competition clause;

7. The preamble to the Constitution has almost entirely been dropped;

8. The competence clause has been further clarified;

9. Article 8c on national parliaments has been added;

10. Application of the new Council voting rules is delayed to 1 November 2014 – and an interim regime will apply until to 31 March 2017;

11. 'Enhanced cooperation' will require at least nine Member States (instead of one-third of them under the Constitution – this could make a real difference if the additional member States join the EU);

12. The 'Copenhagen criteria' are included in the clause on accession.

EARLIER EU TREATIES

Treaty of Nice

The Treaty of Nice, signed on 26 February 2001, entered into force on 1 February 2003. It dealt mostly with reforming the institutions so that the EU could function efficiently after its enlargement to 25 Member States. The Treaty of Nice, the former Treaty of the EU and the Treaty of the EC have been merged into one consolidated version.

Treaty of Amsterdam

The Treaty of Amsterdam, signed on 2 October 1997, entered into force on 1 May 1999. It amended and renumbered the EU and EC Treaties. Consolidated versions of the EU and EC Treaties are attached to it. The Treaty of Amsterdam changed the articles of the Treaty on European Union, identified by letters A to S, into numerical form.

Treaty of Maastricht/Treaty on European Union

The Treaty on European Union, which was signed in Maastricht on 7 February 1992, entered into force on 1 November 1993. 'The Maastricht Treaty changed the name of the European Economic Community to simply "the European Community". It also introduced new forms of co-operation between the Member State governments - for example on defence, and in the area of "justice and home affairs". By adding this inter-governmental co-operation to the existing "Community" system, the Maastricht Treaty created a new structure with three "pillars" which is political as well economic. This is the European Union (EU).

Single European Act (SEA)

The Single European Act (SEA), signed in Luxembourg and the Hague in 1986, and entered into force on 1 July 1987, provided for the adaptations required for the achievement of the Internal Market.

Merger Treaty

The Merger Treaty, signed in Brussels on 8 April 1965 and in force since 1 July 1967, which provided for a Single Commission and a Single Council of the then three European Communities.

Treaty of Rome

The Treaty of Rome, establishing the European Economic Community (EEC), signed in Rome on 25 March 1957, and entered into force on 1 January 1958. The Treaty establishing the European Atomic Energy Community (Euratom) was signed at the same time and the two are therefore jointly known as the Treaties of Rome.

Other Treaties

Treaty establishing the European Coal and Steel Community The Treaty establishing the European Coal and Steel Community (ECSC), which was signed on 18 April 1951 in Paris, entered into force on 23 July 1952 and expired on 23 July 2002.

Moreover, the founding treaties have been amended on several occasions, in particular when new Member States acceded in 1973 (Denmark, Ireland, United Kingdom), 1981 (Greece), 1986 (Spain, Portugal), 1995 (Austria, Finland, Sweden), 2004 (the Czech Republic, Cyprus, Estonia, Hungary, Latvia, Lithuania, Malta, Poland, Slovakia and Slovenia) and 2007 (Bulgaria and Romania).

Based on the Treaties, EU institutions can adopt legislation, which is then implemented by the Member States. To see the full texts of EU legislation, please consult Eur-Lex, the portal to European Union Law. The texts published in the Official Journal (EUR-Lex) are the only authentic versions.

Forum Contact Address

National Forum On Europe
State Apartments
Dublin Castle
Dublin 2
Tel.:   01 - 670 5900
Fax.:   01 - 670 5877
Email: info@forumoneurope.ie
Web: www.forumoneurope.ie